MY BROTHER'S KEEPER:
Relearning to Live with PTSD

By
Jeremy Scharlow

WORDS MATTER
P U B L I S H I N G
OUR WORDS CHANGE THE WORLD

Words Matter Publishing
P.O. Box 531
Salem, Il 62881
www.wordsmatterpublishing.com

ISBN 13: 978-1-953912-03-9

Library of Congress Catalog Card Number: 2020919732

TABLE OF CONTENTS

FORWARD

Post-Traumatic Stress Disorder (PTSD) is real. Those suffering from it experience a host of symptoms: some are common with all who suffer and some symptoms are unique to each individual. It is never cured but it can be managed. Not all who suffer from PTSD find the means to learn to cope with their symptoms and suicide rates are high for this population.

The silent sufferers are the loved ones who surround the person with PTSD. As a mother of a son and the wife of a husband, both with PTSD, I have had to deal with their symptoms right alongside them. I would venture to say that the stress it has created in my life as I try to help them through an episode is life-altering.

Whether it be to try to calm them down during an irrational and extraordinary fit of rage, to hold their hand to let them know they are loved, to try to convince them that life has so much more to offer or to literally walk behind them in large gatherings so they know someone has their backs, the loved one must always be attuned to their emotional needs. One finds themselves placing their personal needs behind the needs of their loved one who is suffering from the disorder.

I cannot count the sleepless nights I have spent pacing the floor because my son didn't answer his phone for three days in a row. He lived two states away so I could not just pop in to do an in-person wellness check. I was always afraid that this was the time that he had given up the battle and killed himself. Or worse yet, I feared his suicide attempt failed and he was lying on the floor in severe pain due to a debilitating injury to himself.

I cannot count the number of car rides I have made to get away from the uncontrollable anger my husband would experience, for reasons as trite as that his favorite shirt was not clean for him to wear. I couldn't stop the fits of rage but I could escape them. Sometimes I would ride in circles for an hour until I was sure he had time to calm down. I couldn't escape my son's rage, however, because he would rant at me over the phone, saying sometimes horrible and hurtful things to me. But if I hung up on him, how could I live with myself if knowing that he felt even his mother didn't want to listen to him, and it became the catalyst that put him over the edge and he killed himself. So I would listen and cry silently until his anger was spent.

With patience, time, therapy, and love they have both managed to reach a point where their symptoms are manageable on a day to day basis. But as someone who loves them, my fear is still constant. Every day I listen to their words, the tone of their voice, and watch for the tell-tale signs that they are going to have an episode. I temper my words to avoid sending them over the edge. I avoid doing anything that I fear will elicit a negative response on their part. And, I pray several times daily for God to give them the courage and strength to handle their inner battles and to overcome them.

~ Deborah Masegian

Chapter 1
BANG, BANG!

Saturday, May 7th, 2016, I had just gone through the drive-through to get dinner when my shift partner decided to make a traffic stop. I was irritated. It was about 30 minutes before the end of my shift, I was hungry, and had politely suggested many times before that he not make stops so near shift change. Each time I did so, he would joke about how I would get overtime and it was not a big deal. On most days, come end of a shift, I simply wanted to go home and these types of stops regularly ended in arrests which would then require I work overtime. Today, I was relieved when he quickly notified dispatch that he was "code 4" and did not need a second officer. I ate my meal in peace. Shortly thereafter, I heard him end the traffic stop. He told our dispatcher he had only issued a warning. I thought nothing further of it.

After finishing my dinner in a small parking lot near the edge of town, I headed back to the police department for shift change. I was anxious to get out of work because I had made plans with a couple of friends and we were going to meet to see a movie. I drove back to the police department, happy my partner's traffic stop did not turn into anything major, and I would be ending my shift on schedule.

With only about 10 minutes remaining in my workday, I approached the police department from the east, heading west on Oak Street near Vine, I saw a vehicle turn toward me from the intersection, two blocks ahead. The vehicle did not have its headlights illuminated. I remember thinking, "Well shit, can't very well say I didn't see that," as the vehicle passed me in the opposite direction, headed east.

I turned my squad car around to try to catch the vehicle. The stop my partner had just completed was in the same general area and I wanted to ensure I was not addressing the same issue for which he had just issued a warning. I asked him, over the radio, why he had stopped the other vehicle. My partner told me he stopped the vehicle because it did not have any illuminated taillights. He also informed me the driver of the vehicle was extremely agitated. Based on the description of the vehicle and the reason for the stop provided by my partner, I knew this vehicle not to be the same as the one he stopped.

As I turned my squad car around, I saw the vehicle turn south on Vine. I caught up to the vehicle, just as it pulled into a driveway on the east side of the road. The vehicle was now safe in the driveway, so I thought I would engage in some "community policing" and not take enforcement action. I rolled down the window to let the driver know his lights were not functioning. Unfortunately, someone else had a different plan. As I rolled down the window to speak with the driver, I heard a second man yell, "Fucking Scharlow."

I immediately thought, "Oh shit." I had no idea who was yelling at me or why, but the words spoken and tone immediately told me I was not safe. Was this someone I had previously arrested? I had just worked a case in which a person offered a car and $1000.00 cash to kill me.

I saw the driver of the vehicle I had followed, still in his vehicle in the driveway. I then saw a second person from the opposite side of the driveway. He was now running toward me. I opened my squad car door and tried to get out. As I tried to get out of my squad car, he was upon me. I was able to stand but was trapped between the open door and the door frame of the car.

I put my right arm up to stop the person from coming at me. I felt his chest touch my hand, followed by blows to the top of the head as he began punching me. I used my left arm to block the punches as he continued, blow after blow. I moved toward him, trying to decrease the distance to lessen the force behind the strikes and I tried to radio for help. The scuffle caused the dial on my radio to move and change the channel muting my cries for backup. All of this occurred in a matter of seconds.

Still unsure of why I was being attacked or by who, I deployed my Taser. I saw both probes strike the man punching me, in the chest. It had no effect. I instantly remembered a Taser has two modes, drive stun and probe deployment. Although the probes failed to create a connection allowing for muscle interruption, I knew I could use the drive stun mode to cause pain and stop the attack. I pushed the Taser into his chest and pulled the trigger. The Taser was effective, causing pain, and allowing me to push my attacker off me. I created distance from him and my squad car. I backed away yelling, "POLICE, STOP!"

I saw the man who had just attacked me, reach into his pocket and pull out a black handgun. Before I could react, it felt as though I had been struck in the right arm with a sledgehammer. I knew instantly I was shot. My arm burned, my hand tingled, and I could see the blood, but my hand still functioned.

Without thought, I drew my pistol with my injured arm and returned fire. My next memory is my taking a knee to reload as my slide locked back on my pistol. I looked up as I reloaded, and I saw the man get up from the ground and run into a nearby house. I began looking for cover.

Although I was injured, I knew I could not let him escape.

I also knew I needed help! I ran toward my squad car when I remembered the only parts of a vehicle that would stop gunfire were the engine block and potentially the wheel hubs. Looking around, I instead found a brick façade building directly adjacent to the house the suspect had entered. I took cover behind the building. From here I thought I could begin to set up a perimeter. I also took the opportunity to check my wound.

I could see I was bleeding heavily. My Glock 23 was covered in blood. My arm throbbed and tingled. It now felt as though I had been hit in the funny bone with a hammer. Luckily my hand still functioned. I saw a gaping hole in my right forearm, just below my wrist. I notified my dispatcher, "METCAD 6g22, shots fired, I'm hit," as I took a position allowing me to see the entry of the residence. No response.

I was in disbelief when I saw the man exit the house with an AK-47. I thought to myself, "My pistol isn't going to win that fight" and I hid back behind the brick building. I heard multiple rounds fired from the rifle. I was unsure if he had seen me or what he was shooting at. I again went over my radio, "METCAD 6g22, shots fired, I'm hit." This time, everyone heard me!

The night shift officer who was to relieve me was arriving at the police department as this occurred. I saw her taking cover behind vehicles in the police department parking lot. She began yelling for me to come to her. Although I wanted to set up a perimeter to keep the suspect from escaping, I knew I was out-gunned and wounded so I retreated to her position. She began checking me for other injuries. In doing so, two of her fingers went into the wound in my arm. I began feeling dizzy and tired. I wanted to sit down. I asked the night shift officer if I was all right. She responded saying, "Yeah, you're good."

I at once felt a boost of energy. I redrew my pistol and started back to reengage the suspect. Before I could move positions, the night shift officer stopped me saying, "You're not that good."

A third officer arrived on scene to the south of our location. Unfortunately, the suspect was able to get into a vehicle, ram my squad car, and escape the area. We were unable to maintain the perimeter, he got away. The night shift officer and I got into an unused squad car and she evacuated me to the local fire department where my treatment began. A short time later, I arrived at the hospital where multiple officers from multiple agencies had already gathered. They were there to offer their support and ensure I felt safe. It would be the only time the local policing community showed me support.

I was released from the hospital early Sunday morning. Although I do not recall, based on the way the wound presented, I had put my arm up to cover my face, as if my arm could stop the bullet. The round had gone in near my elbow and exited near my wrist in my forearm. The bullet traveled the length of my arm but did not strike bone or any major veins. I was sent home with the wound packed in gauze and Ibuprofen for pain.

My clothes, my cellphone, my gear, and my weapon were all seized as evidence. My injuries were photographed and I was ordered not to speak about the issue until I was formally interviewed by the State Police. I complied. Upon arriving home Sunday, friends and family surrounded me. I felt energized like I could do anything. Although I had not slept in over 20 hours, sleep was not an option. I was alive!

Chapter 2
ALIVE

Sunday was a blur. I was unable to sleep and many people stopped by, called, or messaged, all wishing me a fast recovery. Every time the doorbell rang, I feared it may be my attacker coming to finish the job. This went on all day.

Sunday night, exhaustion finally won out. My arm throbbed with pain, but I slept better than I had ever before. It was restful sleep. I woke up the next morning elated. I felt like I had unlimited energy and I could conquer the world.

The .380 caliber round made a very small entry wound which I covered with a Band-Aid. The exit wound, on the other hand, left a gaping hole in my forearm approximately two inches long; one inch wide, and about a half-inch deep. This wound needed debridement (removing of damaged tissues through scrubbing), packed and dressed two times a day. As one would assume, this caused excruciating pain and I was unable to do it by myself at first.

For the first three days, I was able to rely on a paramedic friend, but he soon became "unavailable" when I would ask. My girlfriend at the time was too squeamish and was unwilling, so I asked the only person I could, my daughter, Ariel.

Ariel was 16 at the time. I became a police officer when she was about five years old. The police academy I attended was a three-month, live-in program. Ariel's mother and I had joint custody, but Ariel usually spent six weeks every summer with me. I was at the police academy when she was supposed to stay with me, so my ex would bring her to see me almost daily.

When asked, Ariel has fond memories of coming to swim with me at the hotel I was staying at through the duration of the academy. (the dorms were full, and I got a hotel room by luck of the draw). But this is also when she started asking me questions about me being a police officer.

"Daddy, what happens if you get shot?"

I knew this was a possibility, however rare, associated with my job but I did not want my daughter to live with this fear. Instead of explaining probability and statistics to a five-year-old, I harmlessly made a joke out of it. Each time she asked I would respond, "Don't worry baby, I'm bulletproof."

Now, I sat here with a bullet wound in my right arm and no one to rely on but her. The moment I asked for help, I broke into tears, but she did not hesitate to help. My 16-year-old daughter who cried if she got a shot at the doctor's office, got dizzy if she saw blood, and refused to go fishing with me any longer because it hurt the fish, put her own fears aside and properly took care of my injury. She came by twice daily to treat my wound until I was able to care for myself.

Of course, because she is my daughter, her "smartass" sense of humor had to come out. One day, while removing the gauze from inside my arm and replacing it with new, she said to me, "I told you that you were not bulletproof."

This is the moment I first consciously thought of how close I came to death. Because of one man's rage, I almost lost my life. I would not have gotten to see Ariel grow, get married, have children, meet my grandchildren. This is also the first time I thought about my shooter's two young children. Although my shooter was still alive, his children were now going to be without a father. There were only two options I saw for this man's future, prison or death. In addition, these poor children would have to live knowing their father had tried to kill a police officer.

During these first few days, people were coming and going. Everyone I knew was calling or stopping in to see how I was. The rest of the first week was a blur. The suspect who shot me was still at large and the FBI now offered a reward for his capture. As the week progressed my fear grew that the man was going to come and try and finish what he started. The man knew my name. He screamed it at me before he attacked me, but now I also knew his.

In August of 2013, I was dispatched to a popular gas station in response to a white male yelling racial slurs and trying to fight a black patron at the gas station. I responded to the gas station and spoke with the victim. He gave a description of the suspect and confirmed the man was yelling racial slurs and telling him to get his "n-word, ass out of town."

Through the investigation, I was able to get a license plate and contact information for the suspect. Using this information, I attempted to contact him at his home so I could try to understand his perception of what occurred.

I pulled into the driveway and exited my squad car. I approached the side door closest to the driveway when I saw the suspect and his wife tending a fire in his back yard. I spoke loudly, as he was some distance away, identifying myself and asking to speak to him. He immediately yelled, "Get the fuck off my property unless you have a warrant," balled his fists and began running toward me. I feared he was going to attack me, so I drew my taser, pointed it at him and ordered him to stop. He complied as he continued to yell obscenities and threats at me. I called for backup and waited. A short time later, a backing officer arrived, and we took the suspect into custody for aggravated assault of a police officer and disorderly conduct. While en route to the jail, the suspect continued to yell in both English and German, at one point stating I was locking up all the "innocent white men and giving the country to those animals."

In a second contact with the man, I had stopped his wife for speeding. She was visibly upset and crying. She explained to me that she and her husband had gotten into a fight and she was headed to her mother's. She denied the incident had been physical, but based on her demeanor I was unsure this was true. I requested assistance from the local sheriff to contact the individual to ensure he was okay as well. A deputy came to my traffic stop to assist me and help ensure no domestic violence occurred. We tried to reach the man via the telephone number provided by his wife. When we called, he yelled at us saying we were not wanted and that he had nothing to say. He refused to answer any questions and hung up. As the wife continued to deny any physical battery, I provided her with domestic violence assistance information and she left the area. We were unable to make contact with the man a second time. Was either of these the reason why this man tried to kill me? I did not know, but I could not stop the questions that circled in my head. Why? What if? I should have done...

As the week progressed, my mind continued to ask questions that I was unable to ignore. I felt like I needed to talk, but I had no one to speak with. I had been ordered not to speak. I reached out to my police department and was again directed not to talk to anyone until after my formal interview. Unfortunately, they did not schedule my formal interview until the following Friday, five days after my shooting. So here I am, a bullet hole in my arm, I had asked to talk to someone and was told to wait.

In 2013, the International Association of Chiefs of Police issued a guideline on how to respond to officer-involved shootings titled, "Officer-Involved Shooting Guidelines." These guidelines are widely accepted across the country as the "best practices" in dealing with a critical incident of this nature. The paper began with a purpose statement:

"It is widely accepted that officers involved in shootings or other significant critical incidents require immediate support. (1) The goal of these guidelines is to provide recommendations to public safety agencies, and the mental health providers who provide the service, to prepare and respond to the health and well-being of law enforcement personnel following an officer-involved shooting" (International Association of Chiefs of Police, 2013).

My administration, either because they did not care or they were uneducated, failed to follow many of these best practices.

After my shooting, my weapons were seized, but I was never provided another; I was never provided information explaining the physical or psychological reactions to shootings; I was denied access to speak with trained peers or other's while I waited to be interviewed; the investigation itself lasted more than a year; and the department had no policies or procedures in place to address any of these issues, including medical retirement or a pension board.

Why was my administration not prepared for the reality of policing? Why were these failures allowed to occur? I had no answers to these questions, but I followed orders and did not discuss my situation with anyone. Instead, I began drinking more heavily. I found comfort in alcohol as it quieted my mind, if only temporarily.

Chapter 3
DOWNWARD SPIRAL

Friday finally came. Nearly seven days after my being shot, I hadn't been able to talk to anyone, and now I was required to speak with two detectives from the Illinois State Police. Any time an officer discharges their firearm in the line of duty, an investigation begins into the lawfulness of the officer firing the weapon. This means I was a suspect in a criminal investigation for shooting another human being.

I arrived at the police department about thirty minutes early. I was immediately greeted by my chief of police. The entire shooting happened in the back yard of the station. My heart raced, I began to sweat, and my hands began to tingle.

I could see the house the man retreated into and the house behind where the man was standing when I fired my weapon. This is when I learned multiple rounds from my weapon went into the home behind where the suspect was standing. I instantly felt ill as I ask my chief about any of my rounds hurting anyone. He responded telling me he believes I hit the suspect in the neck and leg based on blood patterns found in the stolen truck. Thankfully, no one else was injured. Relief...

My chief then escorted me to see my squad car. We entered the garage and I see the door bent all the way forward. The suspect had used his truck to ram the door of my squad car when he escaped. I also saw multiple bullet holes. It was clear, based on the trajectory of the rounds, he believed I had gotten back in my squad car. 7.62 rounds fired from his AK47 went through the driver's seat, the in-car computer, the dashboard, the driver's doors... it was painfully clear the man was trying to kill me.

My chief then escorted me to our "soft interview" room. This is the room I had used for most of my professional career to investigate crimes occurring in the village I had policed. Now, sitting in the same interview room I had used countless times to investigate real criminals, I was being interviewed. The Fraternal Order of Police had provided me with an attorney, but I had only spoken to him briefly prior to the interview. I was scared. Rarely did anyone being questioned in this room, not end up in jail.

The interview lasted over an hour. It was draining. I explained the sequence of events in detail in the presence of my lawyer and two Illinois State Police detectives. I answered all the questions asked of me. I also learned the man believed he had killed me based on statements he made to people about why he was injured and running.

I went home Friday afternoon in shock. I had just learned this man intended to and thought he succeeded in killing me. If he knew I was alive, would he come back? What about his family, would they come after me next? Why did he do this? What motivates a person to take the life of another person? Questions like these circled in my mind. I was unable to quiet them. This is when I experienced my first panic attack. I felt a pain in my chest, my heart was racing, I could feel my blood pressure rising. I was sweating and began breathing very heavily.

Approximately three years prior to this, doctors discovered a congenital defect in my heart prompting the need for open-heart surgery. I had been reporting chest pain for years, but the defect wasn't discovered until I was 33. I feared my heart was failing again. Luckily, my then-girlfriend had experienced panic attacks before and was able to help calm me. This experience alone was terrifying.

Adding to my stresses, I was now on paid administrative leave pending the outcome of a criminal investigation into my discharging a firearm on-duty. Although I knew the legality behind an on-duty shooting, my mind would not rationalize the logic. I began fearing some local politician would try to use my officer-involved shooting as political fodder. I spent many hours going over every possible scenario. Nothing I did could stop the invasive thoughts. Was I to be "thrown under the bus" through this process forced upon me?

The invasive ruminating thoughts began to take over my days and quickly crept into my nights. I began having some of the most horrific nightmares. Anytime I fell asleep, I would hear gunfire, see a muzzle flash, or see his face. When I woke from the nightmare and looked around my empty bedroom, I would see my attacker's silhouette in every shadow. Each nightmare brought a new wave of anger, adrenaline, sweat, and fear. I did not know how to calm my mind.

As the days went on, I became increasingly depressed. Depression, for me, came in the form of an inability to find the motivation or care enough to do anything. I would feel so sad and disenfranchised, that I would begin to honestly believe nothing I did would matter, so why do anything? I was not sleeping due to the nightmares and it began taking a toll.

One afternoon, after being drug out of the house to go on a river tubing trip, I was riding in the back of a friend's truck. Suddenly, I heard gunfire and saw my attacker standing in front of me. Although it was a brief flash, I was positive it was him; I could even smell the gunpowder. I grabbed for my pistol before realizing what was happening. It had felt so real...

Everything I did and everywhere I went reminded me of my shooting. A car backfired; I was ready to hit the ground. I saw my shooter's face in every male stranger on the street. At night, every shadow was his silhouette. I was always on edge, waiting for the next attack, the next ambush, the next person trying to kill me. I feared it could come again at any moment. As the fears continued the nightmares continued to get worse. I was killed nightly in my dreams and I sought ways to end the pain.

I had always been a "drinker," but it had never affected my life before. I was able to manage my alcohol consumption responsibly. My consumption of alcohol never affected my job performance. I considered myself a "social drinker."

Now, however, I did not care about responsibility, I simply wanted the thoughts and nightmares to end. I would binge drink to the point of intoxication, nightly. It was the only way to end the nightmares. Unknowingly, I created a routine that would lead to deeper depression. As I continued to drink, I continued to act more irrationally. I would then feel embarrassment and regret over my behavior which had a negative impact on my self-image. This led to more depression, invasive thoughts, and anxiety. I felt as though I was submerged underwater and was running out of air. No matter how hard I swam, I could not reach the surface. I was drowning.... In an attempt to quench the pain, I again turned to the only thing I knew that could shut it off...alcohol.

The nightly drinking led to daily morning hangovers. These hangovers led me to lie in bed feeling even worse because I could recognize the unhealthy cycle I had created, but I had no idea how to go about correcting it. Alcohol seemed the only way I could find peace, but at what cost?

I spent increasingly more time alone and if I was with people, I was drinking. I began shrinking my world. I would spend days lying in bed with ruminating thoughts attacking me.

"Why wasn't he more accurate?"

"If he would have killed me, I wouldn't be dealing with this."

"Is his family coming to get revenge?"

"Why me?"

"Will God forgive me for shooting another human being?"

I continued living this way until I could not take it any longer. I wanted the pain to end and I could only think of one way to ensure that happened. If I was no longer here, I would not have to deal with the constant pain, the depression, the hangovers, the fear! I put a gun in my mouth that night. I remember tasting the gun oil and thinking it tasted exactly how it smelled. I thought about how much of a failure I was, how I was unable to cope, and how I was not strong enough to handle what many other officers had before. I believed myself weak with no value.

I have thought about that night many times since. How positive I was dying was the only way to end the pain. I still do not know why I did not pull the trigger. Instead of following through, I got drunker and passed out.

I woke the next morning feeling groggy and hungover. I laid in bed thinking about how close I had come to creating a permanent solution to a temporary problem. Yes, I was in pain but just like the gunfight itself, wouldn't this pain end too? I knew there had to be a way, but I did not know how. I knew I needed help, but I did not feel I could talk to my "friends." We did not talk about our feelings and I did not want anyone to know how I was struggling. Only weak people struggle, and I did not want them to think I was weak. In addition, most of those who I thought were friends became alienated due to my drinking and erratic behavior. The calls from people asking if I was okay had all but stopped. I had told too many people I was okay, although I knew I was not.

Chapter 4
GETTING HELP

Having come so close to death by someone else's hand and then my own was sobering (pun intended). Drinking, talking with "friends," and other attempts at suppressing the thoughts and feelings had failed. In my irrationality, I honestly believed death a workable option.

Now, thinking more rationally, I consciously decided I wanted to live. I had been trying to keep my issues to myself and I was failing. I needed help, but how would all this affect my ability to return to work. I was only 35 years old, I had just finished my Bachelor of Business Administration and I was currently working on a Master of Art's Degree in Legal Studies. My dream was my experience and education would lead to a command position within my department. The fear of losing all I had worked for is what stopped me from getting help as soon as the nightmares started, but it was obvious I was "drowning" and without help, I might not make it.

I first sought help from my family doctor. I made an appointment and ensured it was not through workman's compensation so the department would not know. When I met with my doctor,

I was nervous and guarded. I wanted to tell him enough to get help, but not enough where it might affect my job or get me committed. My doctor lived in my area, so he was already aware of my incident. When I explained I was having trouble sleeping and processing some of the thoughts, he was not surprised. I elaborated about the feelings and how they were affecting me daily but stopped short of telling about my placing the gun in my mouth.

My doctor was exceedingly kind and understanding about what I was experiencing but explained he was ill-equipped to do much more as psychology was not his specialty. He suggested medications to help provide temporary relief but demanded I see a psychiatrist to manage this type of medication. After discussing some non-medicinal remedies, breathing techniques, and centering methods, he prescribed me Xanax and referred me to a psychologist for an evaluation. I took the Xanax as prescribed, but I was terrified of going to a psychologist. I was busy trying to suppress everything I was feeling, and I knew psychologists talk...a lot.

I begrudgingly made my appointment and went through the first intake evaluation. The intake technician told me I showed signs of mood disorders such as PTSD, Depression, and/or Anxiety Disorder. After speaking with the intake officer for some length of time, he convinced me to schedule an appointment arguing my mental health was a priority. I left the office feeling unsure and scared about what was to come, but what other choice did I have? I already saw what would happen if I continued to self-medicate and I wanted to live.

I continued using the Xanax as the doctor instructed and it seemed to help when I was not drinking, but I was drinking most of the time. Due to scheduling, I was unable to start my counseling for a couple of weeks. As I waited to see the psychologist, the days and nights went on, as they always did, but I lived in constant fear.

I went to my first session unsure of what to expect. I knew these types of doctors like to talk about all sorts of things and find meaning in the oddest places. I feared he would psychoanalyze me, determine me unfit for duty, and end my career. I was hesitant to talk to him, but I also recognized if I did not seek out change, I would live in constant fear.

The doctor I was set up with was prior military and explained his love for those in my field, stating his brother and father were both police officers. He explained he understood my fears and helped me rationalize any idea or concept I chose to discuss. I found the first session very conversational. He took the time to learn who I was and what made me tick. He did not push for information immediately, rather he listened to what I wanted to say. After the session, I found myself exhausted. It felt good to talk and I found myself pouring out feelings I did not even realize I had. I agreed to more sessions.

Each session would begin the same. The doctor would ask me what symptoms I had experienced since my prior session and we would discuss what may have caused the individual episodes. We would then reason through methods of handling each situation and discuss reframing the emotions associated with the situations. We discussed my fears and the rationality (or lack thereof) behind them. He also introduced me to exposure therapy.

In addition to counseling, the psychologist referred me to a psychiatrist to see if medications may be a way to help treat the symptoms I was experiencing. After seeing the psychiatrist, I was prescribed multiple medications for depression, anxiety, nightmares, panic attacks, and sleep. At one point I was taking eight medications each day to deal with the mental health effects of my shooting.

It only took a couple of sessions before my psychologist told me he believed my symptoms were related to my shooting and that he did not believe there was a "quick fix" to help me. We discussed the treatment options and the length of time they recommend for each type of treatment. He then told me we could do everything the medical field currently recommends for treatment of Post-Traumatic Stress Disorder and its associated symptoms, but in some cases, the best we can do is treat the symptoms. When asked, he was unable to say if he believed we could alleviate all my symptoms or if they would subside enough where I would be able to function "normally."

I was devastated. I did not need medication to function prior to my shooting, yet here I was. I was no longer the man I thought I was. I felt as though I was weak and a disappointment. Again, I thought about all the other officers who returned to duty after their shooting. Why could I not find the same strength? Depression continued and I continued to seek help.

My girlfriend at the time, was no stranger to depression herself. She regularly fought me, arguing I needed to "get up and do something." All I wanted to do was lay around or go drink. One night, a friend of hers was having a retirement party. The party was for a recently retired correctional officer. I did not want to go, and I tried making excuses. She was relentless, telling me I needed to get out of the house or I would waste away into nothing. I eventually agreed to attend when she pointed out that I would know most everyone there, so I had nothing to worry about.

We got to the party a bit later than it started. People were already there, drinking and being loud. I ordered a whiskey from the bar and looked for a place to hide. The girlfriend did not allow it, forcing us to mingle and talk to people at the party. In doing so, I began speaking with another retired officer from a neighboring department. We had worked a couple of calls together, including his last officer-involved shooting in which he was shot at during a pursuit and stand-off. He asked how I was doing. I responded with the canned answer, "I'm okay."

I thought he would just move on like most others. Instead,

he began talking about how he had nightmares and how alcohol seemed like it was the answer, but it really was not. The retired officer was well-known in our area for being a big physical fitness proponent, having appeared in fitness videos sold internationally. He began talking to me about physical fitness, not as a means of getting in shape, but as a means of working through my depression and anxiety. He suggested that by working out daily, I could release endorphins that would help me overcome the negative ruminating thoughts that filled each day. After a few more drinks and some more battle stories, he convinced me to join him at his gym.

I began working out with him in October of 2016. We would work out together Monday, Wednesday, and Friday. The workouts were about an hour long. There were usually about three or four other people at the gym with us. I knew nothing about fitness, but I did not need too. Each workout would be written on a board prior to my arrival and I would just do what everyone else did. I could barely do 10 pushups at this point and I weighed close to 226 pounds. For a 5'8" male, I was obese.

Within weeks of going to the gym, I began noticing a difference in my daily mood. On days when I would work out, I experienced a decrease in negative ruminating thoughts and when they did attack, I was better able to reason through them. I also found myself more tired by the end of workout days and between the exhaustion and medication, I was able to find restful sleep. The biggest benefit, I drank less because I knew I could not be hungover if I wanted to avoid a verbal lashing for not being able to keep up. It also helped that I was losing weight, I looked better and felt better than I had in a long time. I began setting weight loss and exercise goals and as I met them, I felt a feeling of accomplishment and success. I felt happy again.

With my new appreciation for physical fitness as a means of managing my mental health, I went from working out three days a week to five days or more a week. When I did feel down and I tried skipping a workout, the "gym guys" would harass me until I came and joined them. They did not listen to excuses. Each of us was expected to be at the gym each morning and if we were not, someone else from the group would go drag them out of whatever hole they had dug themselves into. After a few months, it was no longer a question of if I was going to work out on any particular day, but a matter of when and how hard.

While working out helped tremendously, it was not the end-all-be-all. I was able to find some relief from daily depression, anxiety, and other stressors; however, each day the feelings remained, looking for an opportunity to take over my mind and fill my head with negativity. Sometimes, the negativity was too much and when it was, I would turn back to alcohol.

Chapter 5
RELAPSE

It had now been months since my shooting and my doctors released me to return to work from the physical injuries, saying I had recovered. I still had pain in my arm, an inability to fully rotate my wrist, weakness in my grip strength, and numbness and tingling in my hand. The doctors did not believe this was enough to stop me from working.

My mental health status was a different story. The nightmares continued and although they were not as frequent, I often found myself unable to wake. The sleeping medication made it more difficult for me to wake, even when experiencing a nightmare. I felt as though I was trapped living the nightmare. This led to an increase in my depression and nightmare medications. My panic attacks were only occurring about twice a week now, but when they did occur, I was rarely able to shake them. I continued to see my psychologist and we continued his methods of Exposure Therapy (a method of systematically exposing an individual to their trauma in order to "normalize" it) and Cognitive Behavioral Therapy (a method of changing the thought patterns behind one's trauma's and in doing so change the way they feel).

My department was beginning to ask when I thought I could return to work. I repeatedly explained that I was not sure because the doctors could not tell me. Each time I asked, my psychologist would tell me it was too early to tell but he thought I was making progress. He also was not ready to say when he believed I would "peak" in terms of recovery. While I was making "progress," my fears of dying in a police car, my nightmares, my depression, and anxiety still raised questions about my ability to function as a police officer. The doctors managing my mental health were not comfortable saying I was fit for duty but were also not comfortable saying I could not make further progress.

I felt stuck between a rock and a hard spot. I could not file for an on-duty medical disability pension because the doctors were uncomfortable saying I would not make any more progress but they were also uncomfortable saying I could return to work. My department was pressing me to either return or file disability paperwork, but I could not do either without the doctors okay. This went on for months as I continued to follow the doctor's orders and relay the information to my chief. I lived in limbo.

Adding to my fears, I was jolted out of my stagnated life by the receipt of a letter from the police department's workman's compensation insurance. I felt sick. They had decided that I had healed from my injury and requested a mental health evaluation to determine if I truly suffered from Post-Traumatic Stress Disorder. Someone at the insurance company had reviewed my injuries and decided that the mental health injury I was dealing with was not work-related and therefore they were contesting my injury.

After never having a mental health issue and passing a psychological evaluation to become a police officer, this insurance company was now telling me my injuries were not related to someone trying to kill me during an ambush. I did not understand. I spoke with my attorney and she suggested this was customary practice for workman's compensation insurance companies to avoid paying for an injury. This news brought a resurgence in symptoms and new anxieties. Now I had to worry about being paid workman's compensation while I tried to recover from being shot while protecting my community. As required, I went to the appointment for the evaluation. I felt physically sick as I entered the building. I was required to take hours of tests, much like the psychological evaluation I took at the beginning of my career.

Although I had taken the exams in late September, My biggest fear came true on April 3, 2017, when their doctor indicated I did suffer from Post-Traumatic Stress Disorder, but it was not likely due to my shooting incident as much as other traumas in my life. This was accompanied by a letter indicating the insurance company did not believe my injury to be work-related as per their doctor and they stopped paying my salary. I was in horror. How was I going to live?

I called my chief of police in panic. I explained the letter I had received, and he told me he was aware. He went on to explain that the village, per State of Illinois law, must pay an officer's wages for one calendar year while they recover from an on-duty injury, regardless of any workman's compensation insurance. He further explained the village would continue to pay me until that year ended, at which point I would need to either go on disability or return to work.

While thankful the village was required to pay me for at least a couple more months, all I could think about is my doctor's refusal to state I could not make any further progress, the standard needed to begin the disability pension process. In April of 2017, nearly a year after my shooting, my doctor finally told me he believed I could not make further progress and mitigating my symptoms was the only course of action. He then agreed to complete the paperwork needed for my retirement. I began the process immediately, applying for an on-duty medical disability.

I did not have to wait long before I received my next bit of news. On May 5ᵗʰ, 2017, two days shy of a year from the day I was shot, the chief of police called me and asked me to meet him on the outskirts of town. I agreed.

When I met with him, he asked how I was doing. I explained things were tough, but I was managing. He then handed me a termination letter and requested my badge. After being shot in the line of duty and suffering the physical and mental effects of the incident, the department fired me because I was unable to return to work.

I was now without pay and the retirement pension was not in sight. I did not know what to do or how to act. I was in shock. My entire life turned upside down because this individual decided to ambush me. As weeks passed, the nightmares increased, the panic attacks became more frequent, and with that, the drinking increased. Since I had started taking my medications and working out, I had all but quit drinking. But now, the medications seemed to fail. I was unable to quiet the anxiety and fear.

I did whatever I could to escape the memories of my shooting. But no matter what I did, I could not occupy my mind with anything other than my shooting and what had happened in the aftermath. I could not handle the pressure any longer, so I began to travel. Unfortunately, my reliance on alcohol would catch up to me before I got too far.

Originally, I had hoped leaving the area where I was shot would help me cope. It did not help. I now found myself alone, with no one I knew, and nothing to do, except drink.

I found myself in a rural bar hundreds of miles away from where I lived. Being so far from home, I never expected someone would recognize me. After my shooting, my picture was in all of the local papers, TV, and even some national news outlets. I felt as if I could not go anywhere. I hoped being so far from home,

I would feel more comfortable and able to let my guard down a bit. So I did.

I was shocked when I heard him.

"You're that cop that got that guy killed in Illinois, aren't you?"

What did this man just say? Did I hear him correctly? I checked with a friend I was with and she confirmed what I had heard. I instantly felt fear. How did this man know me and how did he know about my shooting? Worse yet, he did not sound very friendly in the way he asked the question. I stood up and was ready to fight. I balled my fists and stepped toward the man who sat across the bar.

Already a bit tipsy, I approached him and asked him to repeat what he said. He stuttered and began backtracking, saying something about how he just meant I was the police officer involved in the shooting. My reaction had already given me away. My anger had the best of me. I confronted the man yelling him down until he apologized. I went back to my barstool and sat with my friend. The man who I just confronted apologized again and began sending over shots. After the third shot of whiskey, he began questioning me again about the shooting again. I stood up again to address the issue and my friend suggested we leave. I agreed, but in my drunken unreasonableness, I did not think about driving. At one of the lowest moments in my life, I found myself arrested for driving under the influence of alcohol.

I returned home more depressed than when I had left. I felt like I had let everyone I knew down. Workman's compensation challenged the Post-Traumatic Stress Disorder claim allowing them to stop paying my wages; I was fired as a police officer because I couldn't return to work and the pension board had not taken action on my pension.

This continued for months and as it continued my depression and anxiety worsened. I found myself not wanting to get out of bed. The simplest tasks seemed overwhelming. I found keeping my relationships with my gym buddies and my girlfriend increasingly difficult.

Although I had received a couple of advanced payments against my eventual settlement with the workman's compensation, the amount was not enough to cover all my bills. As time went on and my financial situation became increasingly strained, I became more depressed and angrier. The anger was so deep and strong. I wanted to smash things and sometimes I did. I would get angry and flip the couch or throw items putting holes in my walls. The outbursts were always violent. I found controlling my anger was impossible, especially if I drank.

As the bills piled up, I began falling behind on my house payment. I had not spoken much publicly about my issues, mostly due to embarrassment. In November of 2017, I had to swallow my pride and I created a Gofundme.org account to help. The account raised approximately $2500.00. While helpful and endlessly appreciative, this was not enough to keep the bill collectors quiet for long. The mortgage company started floating words like "restructure" and "foreclosure."

In addition, my relationship with my girlfriend was strained. On more than one occasion, I had squeezed her too tightly or woken up violently. She no longer allowed me to hold her when we slept out of fear I would unintentionally hurt her. Holding my significant other at night was something very important to me and I could no longer do it because she feared me. In dealing with these issues, in addition to my anger and irrationality, we were unable to properly maintain a workable relationship, so we agreed to part ways.

I remember wondering how much worse it could get. I was again thinking about death regularly, postulating it may have been an easier alternative than what I was currently experiencing.

I needed to find a way to speak about my pain or else I feared it would consume me.

Chapter 6
THINGS ARE LOOKING UP

I had met Jessica at my friend's gym. It was now January of 2018 and we had been dating for a couple of months. I felt a connection to Jessica instantly. She was fit, attractive, intelligent, kind and funny. She listened and allowed me to speak to her without judgment. She seemed to understand what I was dealing with. She shared her own experiences dealing with bipolar disorder and overcoming an addiction to alcohol. I felt a strong connection immediately.

She too preached the mental health benefits of physical activity, the gym, meditation and reading. She encouraged me to refrain from drinking, and she pressed me to build a healthy routine to help me manage my anxiety and depression. I had already recognized the importance of building a routine to help manage these issues as my doctor and I discussed it at many of our sessions. I had also read multiple books arguing the same. While I had a firm grasp of these concepts, I found acting on them incredibly challenging.

When Jessica came into the picture, she taught me HOW to create a healthy routine. She showed me the concepts in action.

Through her own battles, Jessica had developed survival techniques which included using all the concepts my doctors and my readings detailed. She took an abstract concept and walked me step by step through the process of creating my healthy routine. She did it in a way that was not overwhelming. Instead of making profound changes to daily life at any given time, she encouraged setting small attainable goals. Goals so small, they did not even seem like goals.

For example, when Jessica first began coming around, the only time I would leave the house was to go to the gym or the bar. Although my drinking had substantially decreased, she encouraged a further decline without saying a word. She helped me build a daily routine which naturally did not include the use of alcohol. Furthermore, when I did use alcohol, she did not allow my hangover feeling to be an excuse to be a dick or refrain from keeping my routines. This meant 5 am workouts almost every day. Through encouraging my commitment to a healthy physical body, she was also encouraging a discontinuation of a negative coping mechanism, without any negative stigma some may attach to programs aimed at the same goal.

As days went on, Jessica and I continued to build my routines, piece by piece. First, she encouraged me to work out daily. As mentioned above, this had the benefit of decreasing my alcohol intake even further than I already had. I found the harder I worked out, the better I felt. When my anxiety would overtake me, I would go for a run. When I began feeling like I hand nothing to live for, I would go to the gym. When I did not feel like I was making any progress in my life, I could look to the only thing I could control, my physical self. This line of thinking lead me to the conclusion that when life feels as though it has been stripped from you finding a locus of control is important. What was the only thing I believed I had control of in my life? My physical health.

As I continued these routines, my desire to stay home decreased. When we first started dating, Jessica would recommend hiking, running, or walking, and I would scoff at the idea. I was fat. I weighed 225 pounds. I was a "fat kid." Running, hiking, and walking hurt so I was not inclined to do it. Especially after being worn out from the workouts.

The exhaustion from working my body also helped with my sleeping issues. Using a combination of medication and a healthy routine, I was able to get more quality sleep and near-nightly nightmares began to subside.

Unfortunately, as mentioned above, some nights the horrific dreams would break through the medications and I would be trapped within my dreams. The dreams were so real. I could feel the pain, smell the gunpowder, and feel the sweat. Being trapped in a nightmare, but conscious enough to know it is a dream was terrifying. When I would finally wake, I would be overwhelmed with the feelings of fear, anxiety, sadness, and anger.

To combat these emotions in the mornings, Jessica introduced me to motivational speakers and aromatherapy. For some time, she had been telling me how aromatherapy (using essential oils) could have a positive effect on mood by encouraging the release of certain hormones in the body. I did not buy into it and I regularly teased her about it being nothing more than "witchcraft." However, as time went on, I began feeling desperate to find relief. I added both to my morning and nightly routines. Over time, I found that my nightmares decreased. I also found on the mornings I woke from a nightmare I was better able to recover and begin my routine as planned.

Again, Jessica did not just tell me these things worked. She showed me. She began waking every morning 20 to 30 minutes before me to make breakfast and ensure the oil diffusers were running. She did not know which mornings I would wake from a nightmare, so she began doing this daily. She showed me how slight changes over time could become a learned positive emotional response to uncontrollable negative emotions. While I continued to tease the entire process as "witchcraft," I found it incredibly relaxing and helpful in managing negativity.

Unfortunately, this did not end the nightmares. While better able to recover, I wanted to stop feeling the pain I felt with the nightmares all-together. I spoke to my doctors and we adjusted my medications, but this did not seem to help. My Xanax usage increased and on particularly bad days, I would also drink. I did not care how, the pain needed to stop.

Chapter 7
CONTINUED NIGHTMARES

The nightmares, while no longer weekly, were terrible and never the same. I was involved in a shooting in every single one and in every single one, I was hit. I was forced to relive an event that ruined my life. The dreams would always begin peacefully. I may be in a park enjoying a picnic with my daughter or I may be hiking in a beautiful park, but by the end, I was ambushed and shot. Some nights I would wake from whatever horrific dream I was experiencing, and I felt the same burning in my arm as when I was hit almost two years prior. On these nights, I would shoot up in bed, heart pounding, covered in sweat. Sometimes I would sweat so bad I had to change the sheets before trying to return to sleep. Other nights I did not go back to sleep.

I thought the exercise, meditation, talking about my experiences, and the aromatherapy were helping me feel better after an individual episode, but the dreams were still occurring. As the dreams occurred, I found myself falling into a cyclical pattern. I would experience a negative dream and it would cause me extreme emotional distress. For days after the dream, I would feel uneasy and jumpy. The slightest unexpected noise would send me into a panic. This left me very angry and caused me to lash out irrationally to many who surrounded me.

As I recognized my own hypervigilance and my reaction to the situations, I would find myself feeling guilty. I would feel bad about how I had acted, my inability to regulate my anger and emotions, and my inability to handle the situations in front of me. I had always prided myself in acting appropriately/rationally and now, before I could stop myself, I would lose control.

The guilt led to depression. I would begin asking myself things like, "Why couldn't I handle this, I'm not the first person to be shot?" These types of thoughts would become so invasive that they colored my perception of my entire self-worth. I was usually able to work through the depression relying on my medication and routines, but the cycle would begin again after the next nightmare.

Friends and family began suggesting sharing my experience with others may help me better compartmentalize and rationalize my own issues. My doctor agreed that speaking about my issues could help desensitize me to their traumatic effects, essentially a form of exposure therapy. Taking their advice, I began speaking publicly about my experience. I created a Facebook and Instagram account and began talking about my experiences. I was without income as the police department had let me go, I was struggling to keep my bills paid, and I was experiencing troubling nightmares. As I spoke, I found others who were experiencing many of the same things. They would tell me of their nightmares, explaining how they also felt the cyclical pattern I was experiencing.

It was now July 2018. Although a laborious and dehumanizing process, the police pension board ruled my injury an "on-duty disabling injury" in a hearing. Although I had won my pension, the pension board did not have the processes set up to pay the pension, so I was still without any form of income. I reached out to the pension board president (also my union rep) hoping he could help expedite the process. Instead of offing any form of comfort or assistance, he advised me there was nothing he could do and that the process took time. I asked him again for help, pointing out he was also my union rep. He responded stating I was no longer part of the union, so he had no obligation to help me. He then hung up on me.

This threw me into a rage. I was without income, without recourse, and the "brothers" who were supposed to be looking out for me did not care. I took a Xanax to help. The Xanax was not enough, so I took another and another. They did not help. I began drinking.

The following morning, I woke in the hospital. I had faded memories of the voices, being sad, and drunk. I reached out to my "friends" that morning asking what had happened. As I listened to what had occurred, I learned I had gotten intoxicated and called a friend for help. After speaking with him, I ended up calling 911 myself, looking for help. They sent help, however, in my medicated/intoxicated state, I was unable to think or reason clearly.

I cannot express the shame and regret I felt learning how I treated other officers. What I said and how I acted while attempting to refuse to go to the hospital was unconscionable. The "gym guys" disinvited me from working out with them and I learned the "brother" whose gym I was disinvited from, was now dating my ex. In addition, the only other officer to survive a gunshot wound in our county (and one my "gym buddies") gave me an ultimatum. She stated she could no longer be my friend if I refused to go to Alcoholics Anonymous.

I was deeply hurt. I felt abandoned by my police department, my friends, my gym brothers/sisters, and I had alienated myself from most of the local police officers. I found myself in a deep depression. I again did not want to get out of bed, let alone leave the house. For days I would lay around, doing not much of anything…. This was the second time I contemplated suicide.

Chapter 8
FINDING THE THIN BLUE LINE

I had gotten a DUI, was unable to control my behavior and emotions, was dealing with these horrific nightmares, and had completely alienated myself from those who I once considered my support group. I had lost my passion, lost my livelihood, and did not recognize who I was. Through all of this, Jessica stood by encouraging me to refocus and continuously showing me these events did not define who I was. She doubled down on her encouragement of my speaking publicly about what I was experiencing. What did I have to lose?

I was surprised to find a very warm reception from anyone who heard my story. Of course, there were negative police haters, but people seemed to want to hear what I had to say and wanted advice on how I had dealt with the situations I was describing. I saw others feeling the same pain I was feeling and in sharing with them, they expressed gratitude. It felt as though I was helping others again, a feeling I was proud of while being a police officer. For a few moments, I felt good about myself and I wanted that feeling to continue so I continued posting videos and writing about my experiences finding multiple magazines interested in publishing my works.

I refocused my energy on my physical health and recommitted to my routines which had proven effective in improving my daily quality of life. As it was clear the medications and alcohol were a dangerous mix, I recommitted to being alcohol-free. After a lengthy discussion, my doctor and I agreed to adjust the dosage of my medications. This, in conjunction with the routines I had built, quieted the nightmares enough to where I was able to function most days without issue. It worked, most days.

On days where it was not as good, without warning and without any identifiable reason, I would see him. There he was, clear as day. My heart stops and I cannot breathe. The man at the grocery store, it is him, I am positive. I begin to shake, I instantly feel rage, and I want to attack this man. I want to stop the threat. Less than a second passes and just as quickly as I am inundated with these emotions, logic kicks in. The man who shot me is dead and I am safe. I look at the man a second time. His hair is the wrong color, he is taller, and his face was shaped differently. The only similarity was his beard. Months prior, events like these would send me into a deluge of emotions. Now, after countless failed attempts and with the aid of medications, I was able to see logic through the emotion.

I latched on to the logic. I would tell myself things like, "The chances of an individual who is not a police officer being harmed or assaulted is minimal." I read everything I could get my hands on relating to emotional responses. I spoke with my doctors about how to best limit negative or poorly thought out responses to a negative emotion and they provided a number of coping mechanisms, each essentially trying a different way to reach the same goal. The goal of calming the individual to the point where they can think rationally, allowing for an appropriate emotional response. I was teaching myself it was okay not to be in fight or flight mode indefinitely.

Employing grounding techniques in conjunction with the routines, my medications, a supportive relationship, and the benefits I found in speaking with others dealing with similar issues allowed me to begin looking for the positive. I had a family in Jessica and her four daughters, my health was improving daily (I had lost over 20 pounds) and although the nightmares are still an issue, I have learned to use logic through their lies. The depression, anxiety, and hypervigilance continued, but I used all of the tools I had developed over the past two years to improve my daily quality of life. These issues did not go away, but I was learning how to slow down and think before acting. In addition, I felt like I had a purpose in helping others dealing with similar issues, feeding a desire to ensure no other officer suffered similarly. I spoke to this constantly.

One afternoon, Jessica and I had just finished a hike and she was making dinner. I was in my bedroom when I got a message from a representative of Operation Enduring Warrior. They explained they had been watching my story and how I was recovering for some time. The man elaborated further explaining Operation Enduring Warrior (OEW) was a veteran-founded organization aimed at honoring, empowering, and motivating, veterans and law enforcement officers who suffered an injury in the line of duty. I do not recall why exactly, but I had the distinct impression the organization had reached out to me seeking my help in reaching others who suffered from Post-Traumatic Stress Disorder. I agreed to a conference call between me and a couple of decision-makers in their organization. I was instantly excited. I believed I had a real opportunity to be part of helping injured officers who are struggling, find peace. Then it hit me. I was arrested for a DUI and I had acted unconscionably (although medicated and intoxicated). I could not wrap my head around why this organization would want to associate with me. I was a failure.

I decided the best course of action was honesty. I kept my conference call with OEW and after pleasantries, I laid out my situation. I explained my DUI and my recent hospitalization with the belief they would turn tail and run. After ten minutes of portraying myself in the most negative light I could, giving them all of the reasons they should not associate with me, I learned they were there to help me, not the other way around.

The two representatives for Operation Enduring Warrior believed they had the ability to show up where the "Thin Blue Line" had failed me. They asked me to become part of their organization as an honoree, a benefactor of the organization. I was speechless. I was confident I had burned my bridges within the police community locally due to my transgressions and I had assumed it would resonate to all cops everywhere. Instead, both men listened and then shared stories. They told of other officers who were part of their organization struggling with depression and Post-Traumatic Stress Disorder. They spoke about veteran suicide, addiction, and love. Love for our brother and sister who swore the same oath. My failures did not phase these men. After speaking with them, I believed they both saw my pain and for the first time, I felt like someone within the police community cared. They asked me to allow them to honor me at an upcoming event in Kentucky. I accepted their invitation and ended the phone call in disbelief.

I was flooded with emotion. I had been *screaming at the top of my lungs* about the issues I was dealing with involving my police department and from within my own head. I had written countless Facebook posts, created videos, and written multiple articles. The Center for American and International Law's Institute for Law Enforcement Administration even published a study I authored regarding Post-Traumatic Stress Disorder within the law enforcement community. People were listening. Good people who wished to save lives.

Over the next couple of months, I was thrown into the mix with Operation Enduring Warrior. I prepared to compete in the Warrior Challenge Obstacle Course Race in Kuttawa, Kentucky as an honoree. This meant multiple men wearing gas masks to conceal their identity would suffer through the obstacle course with me ensuring I would not fail. The masks kept the men anonymous, ensuring the focus remained on the honoree, while they did everything in their power to ensure the honoree completed the obstacle course. I believe this act represented a larger commitment to the honoree's daily wellbeing and their desire to do anything they could to motivate and empower that individual, on an obstacle course or in life.

While preparing, I did not go two days without some stranger (a member of OEW) reaching out to me with genuine concern over my wellbeing. I had never experienced anything like this. Strangers, all who openly shared intimate details of their trauma, were reaching out to me and every one of them could relate to what I was experiencing. Through these conversations, I began to feel like part of something important. I felt like I was part of a family.

In October of 2018, I completed my first event as an honoree with Operation Enduring Warrior. I have been part of their organization since. The men and women of this organization understand what it means to look out for those who are struggling. Every person in the organization is damaged in some way. Some struggle with issues similar to mine, while others struggle with wartime injuries and amputations. Since my shooting, I witnessed many people claim to want to help create change so no individual suffers alone. These people were the only ones who showed up and demonstrated what it meant to care for others injured while serving our country, instead of just talking about it.

Chapter 9
FULL STOP

It was now August of 2019. I had taken part in two events with Operation Enduring Warrior and was regularly receiving my pension payments. I also received a small workman's compensation settlement, but after deducting the forwarded amounts provided to live after the police department fired me, there wasn't much left. I spent the remainder catching up on bills and ensuring my house was not foreclosed upon.

My medical pension, per law, was awarded at 65% of my final year's wage, but this did not account for overtime. The amount I received was substantially less than what I was used to living on. However, it was tax-free and the department was required to provide me medical insurance, so it was better than nothing. In addition, I could work outside of law enforcement without it affecting my pension payments.

A friend of mine who ran a construction company had reached out to me in January and I had been working for his company as an assistant project manager since. The company was a general contracting firm that built and remodeled stores for a national box store. This job paid well but involved travel. I did not have a driver's license due to my DUI, but as long as I showed up to work on time, my new employer didn't care. I still had nightmares occasionally and regularly fought the anxiety/depression, but I was managing. Jessica and the girls had moved in with me and everything was going well. I had even lined up a new job to start in October of 2019, which paid significantly more and did not involve travel. I was to be a gym teacher at an in-patient behavioral health facility for children.

I was in rural Tennessee when I got the call. My current boss and I were both in the construction trailer when my former chief called. The memory of him firing me sprang to the surface. I was immediately apprehensive. I had not heard from this man in quite a while. I had been vocal about my situation and struggles. He did not seem to think I represented him or the department fairly. I was shocked to see his number appear on my caller ID.

I answered the call with hesitation. I could not imagine what this man had to say to me. He had repeatedly refused to give me the honor of issuing retirement credentials due to fear I would use them to carry a weapon off duty. Apparently, he believed me to be a risk to myself or others. Any time I asked, he would either ignore the topic all together or tell me they have never given retirement credentials in the past, except to a retired chief.

When he began to speak, I could hear it in his voice. Whatever he was about to say was bad. I then listened as my life was destroyed a second time. The chief explained that a reliable source had contacted the police department out of concern for my life. The father of the man who shot me had told the source that the man planned to kill me because he blamed me for his son's death.

I was in shock. Life was just beginning to calm down and I was finding happiness. Instantly, I was angry. I began fervently questioning the chief as to further information about the threat. He told me he did not have any more information than what he had already shared with me. He said the department had consulted the local state attorney and they didn't believe they had enough to charge the man with a crime. The position of the state's attorney was that the threats were within the individual's right to free speech as he made no act of furtherance. The chief stated he only notified me because he felt it his responsibility so I could protect myself.

I was instantly irate. My life was in jeopardy again and the local authorities would not do anything to protect me. My boss, who was present for the call, was also in shock. He immediately pointed out the risk Jessica and the kids would be in should the man try to come get me, especially if I was away traveling.

I ended the call with my former chief and called Jessica. I let her know of the new threat against my life and my fear that she and the kids may all be in danger. Jessica made arrangements for the kids to stay with a family member and drove to Tennessee to get me. Anger and fear were all I could feel. I could not understand why my chief did not have more information and I did not understand why the local authorities were not doing more to keep me safe. He also denied another request to give me retirement credentials.

With these new threats, Jessica and I agreed we could not return with the girls to the house out of fear they would become collateral damage while the man attempted to kill me. My address was not difficult to locate and I could not live under the constant threat. The parents who offered us refuge were more than 500 miles away putting needed distance between my potential killer and myself. I believed the distance a deterrent should he decide to carry out his actions against me. Graciously, my parents agreed to allow us to stay with them while we tried to get established in Michigan. That night, we packed only what we could fit in the car with the four kids and our dog and left Illinois.

The nightmares came back the very first night I stayed at my parents. I was still taking prescription medications which were supposed to allow me to sleep and a second medication for the nightmares but they did little to help. Four or five nights a week I would wake from a nightmare, covered in sweat, with my heart racing. Each night the dreams were different, but they still always involved my being shot. I always woke just after hearing gunfire and feeling the pain. It was very unsettling.

As I tried to cope with the increased nightmares the best I could, I learned my doctor could no longer fill my medications without seeing me. I was taking Duloxetine for depression, Xanax for anxiety, and Trazadone for nightmares. Unfortunately, the village I worked for and which was required to carry my medical insurance, opted for a plan which only had Illinois doctors "in-network." As such, I was unable to refill my prescriptions without traveling back to Illinois, the same area where the new threats against my life originated.

I ran out of Duloxetine first. I expected to feel a change in my mood, but it was the sweating that I felt first. After the sweating came the shakes, nausea and vomiting. I had become physically addicted to the depression medications.

I spoke to my doctor about my concerns, but there was little she could do. She agreed to send me one last script for my sleeping medication and my nightmare medication but insisted she could not continue to fill my prescriptions without an in-person visit. After a long discussion, we agreed to stop my depression medications and allow my body to overcome the physical addiction.

Having had to abandon my home, now addicted to prescription drugs, living in my parents' basement with my girlfriend and her four daughters, unable to find work, and in constant worry about who was going to try and kill me next, my whole personality changed. I stopped working out at the gym regularly, I was short with the kids, I rarely left the basement, and I turned back to alcohol to cope. It seemed like the only way to calm the fear and anxiety, but it let the anger boil to the forefront. I felt angry all the time. When someone looked at me wrong, if someone accidentally bumped me, or if someone interrupted, it was enough to send me into a rage. I became a shell of what I had been. It was as if all the progress I had made since my shooting was gone. I could not shake the constant fear and it was exhausting.

It did not take long before the situation took its toll on Jessica and the girls. The girls did not understand why their lives were completely turned upside down, why they were forced to leave school unexpectedly, leave their friends, and why we could not return to Illinois. They missed their friends, their family, and everything they knew. They had never lived anywhere but central Illinois and they were having difficulties adjusting to life in Michigan. Likewise, Jessica had never left central Illinois and just like with the children, she was finding our living situation unlivable.

As I continued to get drunk, I continued to lose control of my anger and fear. This led to increased hostility toward everyone, especially Jessica. Jessica, unsure of how to help, internalized my anger and hostility as a reflection of how I felt about her. It did not take long before Jessica was unable to take it any further. The stress of the situation became too much. Jessica ended our relationship and she and the children moved back to Illinois.

I lost everything...

Chapter 10
PERSONAL REFLECTIONS

This is where my story currently ends. Although, it is not as much of an ending as it is a pause. An ending implies the situation has resolved itself, yet nothing could be further from the truth. My life is not over, the threats against my life remain, and I continue to struggle with symptoms associated with Post-Traumatic Stress Disorder.

As I reflect over the past couple of years, I am shocked at what I see. I kicked the pill addiction, I lost my family, I had to sell my house, leave the state, and move hundreds of miles away to find safety. All of this after I spent most of my adult life protecting other people's safety. I continued to deal with regular cycles of depression, hypervigilance, anxiety, and nightmares. Never would I have thought this would be my story.

I remain angry. Every night I struggle with sleep or realize I have not left my apartment in days out of fear, I feel it. Every time I hear fireworks, I see a man with a beard like that of my shooter, or someone yells my name, mental images of my shooting and its aftermath flood my mind. This anger consumed me. It cost me everything, including my family. Although continuing to struggle, I have found a few things that have offered comfort and allowed me to continue to move forward.

Firstly, I forgave myself. I realized my shooting and events after the fact, were not necessarily that which I would have chosen given a clear mental state. Of course, I am responsible for my actions, including self-medicating, but these were decisions made under duress when there appeared to be no other option. I need to forgive myself for the continuous invasive thoughts, asking why I was not strong enough to handle a situation other's handle without issue. I need to forgive myself for doubting my own value, thinking myself weak, and planning to end my life.

I feel it important to differentiate between forgiving oneself and absolving one from the responsibility of their actions. Every action we make throughout our lives will affect us in some way. I chose to drink alcohol as a means of self-medication, and I ended up getting a DUI.

Regardless of the situation surrounding my DUI, I made the choice to drive. No action, regardless of reason, absolves one of responsibility. This necessarily means taking responsibility for the substances you put in your body, including those meant to self-medicate.

Secondly, I learned the importance of asking for help and relying on those who offer their aid. As you have read, I did not get much assistance from my police department. The "thin blue line" was non-existent and I was ill-equipped for the emotional aspects of my shooting. Although I was seeing psychiatric doctors, I felt as though my department had virtually abandoned me and this hurt deeply.

It was when Operation Enduring Warrior found me that I found an avenue of support. They have created a network of injured law enforcement officers and military veterans who live BROTHERHOOD. Their only goal is to honor, empower and motivate, those of us who sacrificed in service to our country.

From the firsts phone call to each event I have participated in, to the weekly (sometimes daily calls) Operation Enduring Warrior encourages, they have shown me what it means to support a brother or sister in need. They have provided me with the greatest healing resource of all, the empathetic ear.

Members of Operation Enduring Warrior have listened to me cry, yell, and scream. Many of their volunteers have experienced situations similar to mine (or much worse) and have developed healthy coping mechanisms to help battle many of the issues associated with Post-Traumatic Stress Disorder, anxiety, and depression. When you are sitting alone, lost in your mind, thinking you are alone in the world, remember others have walked our path and survived. You can too! Speaking with those who experienced and/or felt many of the same things I had was more beneficial than I can express in words. It was proof I was not alone and that someone cared!

Thirdly, find something to occupy your time. Although it sounds cliché, "Idle hands are the devil's playthings." Through my years of cycling depression, the ups and the downs, the anxiety, and the fear, I have learned that keeping busy is the most effective way to deter the invasive thoughts.

Keeping busy is different for each person. For me, it involved a daily schedule planned to the hour to ensure I had little-to-no downtime. I found, through trial and experience, that keeping the mind occupied did not negate all invasive thoughts, but for me, it reduced the frequency. I also found myself more able to adjust and get back on track when I had a number of alternate pressing matters on my mind to keep busy. Being unemployed, on disability retirement, and unable to find work, made this difficult. To assist, I began writing and reaching out to others struggling with Post-Traumatic Stress Disorder and the accompanying symptoms. I created a Facebook page, an Instagram account, and created a webpage all aimed at showing others what Post-Traumatic Stress Disorder looks like and how I battle my demons. As time went on, people began reaching out telling me how me sharing my story was assisting them in dealing with their individual struggles. Call it selfish if you like, but I found comfort in believing I was helping others struggling in the same manner I was. I believe this helped because I was able to focus, at least temporarily, on something other than myself. This helped me feel as though I still had value.

Next, I recognized the importance of seeking professional help when I need it. During my struggles, I contemplated ending my life on two occasions. The first, described in this writing, was the catalyst that began my treatment and led to my finding a version of happiness and peace. The second time occurred just a couple of months before I wrote this chapter. While sitting, waiting for things to happen, ruminating on my current and past struggles, I began to doubt my purpose again. In doubting my purpose, I began to question why I am still here and what value I had. On the first occasion, as I described earlier, I put a gun in my mouth and prepared to end my life. I reiterate, I do not know what stopped me that night, but I did not pull the trigger.

On the second occasion, I recognized the feeling of wanting to end my life as irrational. I at once reached out for help. I called my doctors and set up appointments with my psychiatrist and psychologist, I reached out to my brother's and sister's with Operation Enduring Warrior, and I spoke to my parents.

Every person I spoke to listened, including my doctors. Although being enormously proud of my discontinued use of prescription anti-depressants, my doctor and I decided it would be best to try them again. In speaking with my doctors, my family members, and my support system I decided the medications, including anti-depressants were nothing more than a "crutch" used to help me in my recovery. It was no different than someone relying on an actual crutch to lighten the load while waiting for a broken leg to mend. These medications were intended to help manage the depression while I developed new healthy routines and coping mechanisms. They were not meant to be permanent and my doctor took particular care (recognizing my issues with the physical addiction to the last set of prescribed medications) in choosing medications less likely to become an addiction issue.

Finally, although I am still working on it, I am learning the importance of patience. Nothing in the legal and/or mental health system moves fast. There is a lot of downtime or as some like to call it, "hurry up and wait." Each evaluation, each hearing, each step in the process takes time.

While everything takes time, my life was literally placed on hold. I was unable to return to work without the doctor's say-so, I was unable to apply for my pension without the doctor's say-so, I was unable to get a different job without the legal processes being completed.... I think you get the point—nothing moves fast. Unfortunately, during this time, I was left to sit and ruminate over all the possibilities.

The "what-if's" started the day after I was shot. The suspect in my shooting was on the loose and all I could think of was what if he comes and tries to finish what he started? The "what-ifs" continued as the investigation into the shooting went on for months, "What if the prosecuting attorney decides to make an example and charge me with a crime?"

Eventually, like all things, time would answer all my questions. In waiting a week, I learned the suspect who had shot me was killed while they tried to take him into custody. I eventually received official notification that my returning fire was legally justified and I would face no criminal charges. I eventually won my pension. Patience is difficult when your mind automatically goes to the worst possible scenario. This is when I would remember to forgive myself, ask for help, keep busy, and rely on professionals when needed. Eventually, this cycle began to allow me to move forward, instead of continually sitting in negativity.

Chapter 11
SYSTEMIC PROBLEMS

By any measure, the struggles I bore were undeserved. I had sworn an oath to protect my community from those who wish to do others harm and in the process, I found myself severely injured. Through all of this, fear is the single most prevalent emotion I have experienced since the shooting. Fear in many different forms. Sometimes as anxiety, sometimes as depression, sometimes directly in fearing for my safety.

It was fear that stopped me from talking to my command about what I was experiencing. Fear of ostracism, fear of losing my job, fear of the unknown…

A police officer from Texas reached out to me after hearing my story on some social media outlet. He explained he was not physically injured, but through his career, he had experienced multiple traumatic events that were causing him distress. Due to his fear, he did not want to talk to command.

After speaking with friends and family, he began speaking to a counselor. His counselor recommended a temporary duty assignment. Some of the precipitating issues occurred on the shift he was currently working, and they believed the change may help alleviate the distress. This meant he had to discuss it with his command.

Upon discussing the situation with his command, he was put on administrative leave while they ensured he was fit for duty. He eventually returned to work, but how much more distress does having the security of one's livelihood threatened add to whatever other underlying issues they may be experiencing.

Within weeks of being shot, I had received word that our office secretary and a senior officer were overheard laughing and saying how they both thought I deserved to get shot. I brought this information to my chief and was assured it would be dealt with. The officer who stated these things was later promoted.

In another example of "support," nearly two years after my shooting, two of seven sworn officers from my department came to me and apologized for not reaching out and being more supportive. They explained they were directed not to contact me during the pension/workman's compensation cases.

It was known that I did not have a good relationship with either the secretary or the other officer and there are legal reasons behind why these officers were directed not to speak to me, however, this simply exemplifies the toxicity an officer deals with once injured. This is where we need to begin to effect change. Each of us took an oath, swearing to protect our communities, but we then attack one another. Why?

We all put on the same uniform, the same badge, and the same gun. What good does it do to tear one another down? What good does ordering officers not to speak to another officer do, except maybe protect the department's wallet? What message does it send when officers are put under a microscope for expressing distress? What kind of human being laughs and jokes about another officer being shot?…

On the opposite side of the spectrum, I had the opportunity

to speak with a federal officer from the Florida area. This officer was walking through a parking lot when a man screamed about his dislike for the police. The suspect then shot the man in the back multiple times before killing himself.

When speaking to this officer, he explained how supportive his department had been.

The department ensured he had all the necessary tools to ensure he made a full recovery. This officer credited (in part) the handling of his incident with his ability to make a full recovery and return to work.

While recognizing the anecdotal nature of these stories and others shared by officers going through similar circumstances, I find a common theme. In situations in which an officer had a traumatic event (officer-involved shooting, child death, suicide, etc.) there seems to be a correlation with departmental support and an officer's ability to return to work. I believe we have clear evidence there is a correlation, however, more study is needed in this area to determine the magnitude of the correlation. On its face, the concept holds weight.

Unfortunately, I think as my command staff and many others prove, we cannot expect all departments across the country to look out for an individual officer's best interests. These agency heads are tasked with the function of the organization and once you are thought "non-functional," you are no longer of value and discarded like spent shell casings. As such, we can no longer trust those in command positions will do the right thing. Too many times, officers injured in the line of duty struggle like I did. This is unacceptable!

To combat this, we need to enact national legislation aimed at protecting our officers. Any such legislation would first need to define Post-Traumatic Stress Disorder as an occupational hazard associated with law enforcement. This, in combination with pre-employment testing, will allow us to set a baseline by which to determine if an officer's new diagnosis of Post-Traumatic Stress Disorder was related to their employment. If no issues were discovered during pre-employment psychological evaluations, the burden of proof must be shifted to the agencies to prove the injury was not work-related. By shifting the burden of proof, we take the onus off the officer and place it on the organizations. By doing this, we can make command staff and the organizations we work for, take responsibility for the injuries the officer suffers while protecting their communities. This could also stop insurance companies from claiming the injury was not work-related, as they tried to do in my circumstances.

In addition, by shifting the burden of proof to the agencies, we may open the door for officers who begin experiencing Post-Traumatic Stress symptoms without a specific traumatic event to seek assistance for these mental health issues under workman's compensation. This will allow more officers access to mental health resources while reducing the likelihood of the officer being "blackballed" for speaking up.

Finally, as you recall, I was fired from my department due to legislative timelines put in place for injured officers. The law stated any officer who cannot return to work from an injury after one year, may be terminated. In my case, as I explained in previous chapters, my doctors told me that a determination on how one may respond to Cognitive Behavioral Therapy and/or Exposure Therapy as a treatment for Post-Traumatic Stress Disorder cannot always be made within legislatively stated timelines. This can create a gap in income for an injured officer, creating more uncertainty and stress in the life of someone already struggling. Any legislation aimed at protecting our police officers must be updated to fit in terms of medical practice and treatment.

While protecting officers from their command staff is one

avenue to help create a safe and healthy work environment, the toxicity we are subjected too is not only from within. For too long there has been a divide between our society as a whole and our police officers. To see this, all one needs to do is look to the "community policing" efforts launched all over the country to "regain trust" in our police officers.

Everyone we know has a story about how some officer, "fucked them" but rarely do they explain why they were involved with the police to begin with. Nobody wants to take responsibility for their own actions. They instead shift blame any way they can. Combine this with command staff who would rather placate the wrongdoer than protect an officer and we have a perfect mix of toxicity. A toxicity spurring the growing suicide epidemic in the law enforcement community.

To see this brief example, we simply look at some of the ridiculous complaints lodged against police officers. Complaints that originate often, because the individual complaining did not want to take responsibility for their own actions. Instead, they seek to blame the cop.

The village I worked for had a festival called the "River Fest." The festivities lasted about four days every summer. The event, sponsored by the city, had a beer tent that shut down around 11 p.m. on each night. Just like any "beer tent" across the nation, people enjoyed the live music and alcohol to excess.

On this particular night, the younger crowd got themselves liquored up and when the festivities ended, approximately 1000 people packed into two bars in town meant for maybe 100 people apiece. As expected, the over-serving of alcohol and crowds led to problems.

I was called to one of the bars because a couple had gotten into a fight. Upon arrival, I found a female sitting on the front curb crying. She was obviously intoxicated. I made contact with her and tried to ask if she was okay. Immediately, another female (one I had known for many years prior to my becoming a police officer) exited the bar and began interfering. She was also obviously intoxicated and continually ignored orders to let me be and let me investigate the potential domestic situation.

After multiple warnings, I pulled the second female aside and explained that she was interfering, and I needed to investigate a potential domestic battery. She began talking over me and explaining that nothing had happened. I thanked her for her perspective and explained the need to speak with the potential victim without outside influence. I explained that her further involvement would end in her arrest for obstructing as she would not allow me to talk to the potential victim. She became more upset and told me I could not do anything about her talking to her friend.

I again tried to speak to the potential victim and the second female again interjected. I arrested the female and placed her in the back of the squad car. This upset the girl's boyfriend who then wanted to fight me and other officers on scene. His friends were able to get him away from the bar to avoid his arrest while I continued to investigate the domestic situation.

While speaking with the potential victim, I learned that no physical contact had occurred and that no true domestic took place. She wanted to go about her night and leave with her friends and she did so.

As I was completing my interview with the potential victim, the second girl's father showed up. He was about a foot taller than me and easily 100 pounds heavier than me. I saw him approach as he demanded I let his daughter out of my car. He cursed and yelled, telling me he would "whoop my ass" if I did not let her out. Any attempt to interject was met with him yelling over me.

Finally, he looked at me, pointed and said, "If you don't let my daughter out of that fucking car right now, I'm going to do it." I responded, "You touch that fucking car, I will tase you, and you will go to jail with her." He stood down and agreed to pick up his daughter at the police department after she was processed under a village ordinance for obstructing.

The next day, the man who thought it okay to curse and threaten me, filed a complaint arguing I was unprofessional because I cursed at him. My chief called me into the office and wrote me up due to how I spoke to the individual.

In many of the articles I write, I refer to the "war on cops." I speak of a concerted effort to place blame and undermine the professionalism of policing in general. From the NFL to the Black Lives Matter movements being promoted in schools, our society is being inundated with false narratives portraying the police as the catalysts for violence. This is creating a larger divide between police officers and the communities they offer their lives to protect. Regularly these people scream, "we want justice" and what about my "rights" without truly understanding either.

What is "justice?" Merriam-Webster's Dictionary defines justice as, "the maintenance or administration of what is just especially by the impartial adjustment of conflicting claims or the assignment of merited rewards or punishments." (Merriam-Webster, n.d.)

What is a "right?" Again, Merriam-Webster's Dictionary defines a right as, "something to which one has a just claim: such as (a): the power or privilege to which one is justly entitled." (Merriam-Webster, n.d.)

Everyone can agree with these definitions at face value, but once clouded by emotion and a strong belief that the police are your enemy, it can become less clear. Look at the case of Michal Brown in early August of 2014.

According to the media and the Black Lives Matter movements, Michael Brown and a friend were simply walking down a roadway when Officer Wilson, without justification or cause, harassed Brown. An altercation occurred and at some point, Brown put his hands in the air and yelled "don't shoot." Officer Wilson shot Brown, murdering him. As I wrote in an article I had published in a law enforcement magazine, "Before the investigation can get off the ground, there are already screams for justice and the media spins the story, turning Brown into an innocent child singled out by murderous police."

During the course of the investigation, the "hands up don't shoot" narrative was found to be fabricated, yet we still hear this chanted at countless protests aimed at demonizing our protectors. Although the facts proved, unequivocally, that Brown attacked the officer and the officer acted appropriately, this began the "Hand's up don't shoot" and the Black Lives Matter movements. The people riot when they do not see what they perceive as "justice" (Scharlow, 2019)."

Another example occurred in July of 2014. Eric Garner was selling cigarettes illegally when confronted by Officer Pantaleo. Garner resists arrests as Pantaleo and other officers attempted to take Garner into custody for the violation. Shortly after the altercation, Garner died. Again, as I pointed out in a previous article:

"Before any investigation, a video surfaced of Officer Pantaleo using a "chokehold" and Garner yelling, "I can't breathe." Again, calls for "justice" echoed as the people rioted in the streets. Later, according to NBC New York, "NYPD's chief surgeon Eli Kleinman in 2014 found Pantaleo's action was not a chokehold, and that Garner most likely died because of an underlying heart condition. (Scharlow, 2019)."

Both stories exemplify the disconnect between our justice system and society's understanding of their rights and the proper application of justice. It also exemplifies the concerted effort by the media, to paint police officers in the most negative light possible.

The concept of community policing, which began in the

early 1960s is a step in the right direction. Per the DOJ community policing is, "in essence, a collaboration between the police and the community that identifies and solves community problems" (U.S. Department of Justice, 1994). In theory, this idea has promise. Unfortunately, we have collectively failed in terms of executing the concepts in the mission of community policing as defined above. Too often agencies believe a social media campaigns humanizing their officers are all that is necessary to engage in community policing. They allow officers to post silly dancing videos or use social media to brag about officers helping the public outside of enforcing the law. While this type of public relations campaign is necessary, it stops short of addressing the actual disconnect between law enforcement, the justice system, and our society at large.

Instead of playing cute games and showing individual instances of charitable deeds done by officers, we need to really look at the core problem. While well-intentioned, someone seeing a few videos of a few cops doing a couple of good things will not do much to change the hearts and minds of people who feel their individual rights and freedoms are being violated regularly.

Officers around the country engage with millions of people each year. The overwhelming majority of these contacts end without issue. However, some feel such strong hatred for police officers that they push for a collective "war on cops." This war on cops thrives due to a disconnect between our justice systems and society, begin with a misunderstanding of the role and expectations of what a police officer does in our communities.

Illinois Compiled Statutes define police officer (statutorily defined as a peace officer) as follows:

"Sec. 2-13. 'Peace officer.' 'Peace officer' means (i) any person who by virtue of his office or public employment is vested by law with a duty to maintain public order or to make arrests for offenses, whether that duty extends to all offenses or is limited to specific offenses, or (ii) any person who, by statute, is granted and authorized to exercise powers similar to those conferred upon any peace officer employed by a law enforcement agency of this State (720 ILCS 5/2-13) (from Ch. 38, par. 2-13)."

Notice the statute does not define a police officer as a psychologist, a doctor, a lawyer, or substance abuse counselor. Police officers are charged with upholding the laws enacted by your elected officials. In my time handling calls, the vast majority were non-police related.

Late one random night, I was called to a residence because the person's child would not listen to his father about a specific grounding implemented in the household. I met the father on the front stoop of his residence. He explained his child had attitude issues, ADHD, and was bipolar. He further explained that his son was acting up in school and believed his son to be using drugs. As such, he received a grounding as punishment. The juvenile was refusing to abide by the grounding and the parents wanted me to ensure their child listened.

Of the requests made, the only police-related issue was the use/possession of cannabis by a minor, so I first addressed the drug issue. I asked if he had searched his son's room or drug tested him. The father was aghast, arguing this violated the child's rights to privacy. I then asked if he would allow me to search the room for drugs. He seemed shocked at my request and promptly denied it. A lengthy conversation ensued. During our lengthy discussion, I offered many suggestions including the recommending counseling options and/or the Department of Child and Family Services. Eventually, I explained the child violated no law other than the potential drug issues and the police could not force a child to do something the parents were unwilling to do themselves. I further explained I could not fix 14 years of questionable parenting in an hour. This was met with anger, I was asked what their taxes paid for, how I thought I was being a community servant, and then asked to leave (I did so happily).

This father had an unreal expectation of what a police officer's job included. He thought I would come into his house and bark an order at his child and the child would obey. His inability to take responsibility to parent his child was transferred to me and when I refused to play, he attacked my position. Police only have the ability to act within the law. Laws we enact as a society for the community good. The police officer does not make the law, only apply the law as your elected officials have directed. When people have expectations otherwise, they are rarely happy with the results.

Another example we see regularly occurs each time some suspect refuses to get out of a car or roll down their window. While doing this they regularly make claims to "know my rights." They say this without knowledge of Supreme Court Cases like Pennsylvania v. Mimms.

In Pennsylvania v. Mimms, an officer stopped a subject for driving with expired license plates. The officer asked the suspect to get out of the car and produce his driver's license and registration for the vehicle. While doing so, the officer noticed a bulge in the suspect's jacket pocket. The area was known to be violent and heavy in drug use and gangs. For his safety and because he believed the bulge to be a weapon, he frisked the suspect finding a loaded revolver. The suspect was indicted and convicted for carrying a concealed weapon and unlicensed firearm *Pennsylvania v. Mimms, 434 U.S. 106 (1977)*.

The suspect believed the officer overstepped his legal authority in ordering him out of the vehicle. He appealed his conviction, eventually landing in the United States Supreme Court. The Court held, "The order to get out of the car, issued after the respondent was lawfully detained, was reasonable, and thus permissible under the Fourth Amendment *(434 U.S. 106 (1977))*."

How many of these videos end with an officer breaking the window and pulling the suspect out?

Most people believe what they have seen in movies, television, the mainstream media, and social media. They believe their friends' and families' interpretation of what law is, but often they are ignorant of their actual rights and/or responsibilities. Society, as a whole, is even less educated in case law—a body of law dictating almost all actions in which an officer engages.

This is where we can affect the most change. I believe the disconnect stems from expectations not being met due to an incorrect social expectation incorrectly placed on our police officers. Said another way, people are calling a plumber to fix their electrical and then get angry when they are told the plumber does not do electrical work. The officer is placed in a no-win situation before they even respond to the call.

This leaves us two options. First, we can train our officers to be phycologists, drug counselors, marriage counselors, and the like. Unfortunately, I believe this extremely burdensome, expensive (the education requirements alone), and not sustainable. While I believe training our officers is important, I do not believe we can expect individuals with these types of educational requirements to agree to work on public service salaries. The troubles with this choice are further compounded by the "Defund the Police Movement." Multiple studies and common sense suggest a correlation between the funding of police and the crime rates. As funding and police activity is reduced, violent crimes increase.

Our second option, one in which I believe we could affect the most positive change, is to educate our populace on their rights and responsibilities under the law. Individual departments can begin without any direction from state or other officials.

The University of Illinois Police Department did this very well. The University police department coordinated with all of the other local police agencies and organized a yearly Citizens Police Academy. This program lasted a couple of weeks and was broken into sessions covering specific topics. As part of SWAT, I assisted in demonstrations as we educated the public about our actual job functions. We spent time explaining certain tactics, allowed people to see our equipment, explain how we used the kit, and why. Other sessions included topics such as criminal law, traffic stop enforcement, etc. The most important aspect of the academy was it allowed the citizenry to ask questions directly to the officers in a non-confrontational environment.

It would not be difficult to create a course on constitutional rights and responsibilities as it pertains to interactions with our law enforcement. This concept could be extrapolated to high school courses, community center trainings, HOA trainings, driver's training programs, or even online outreach programs. Any such program MUST address an individual's rights and re-sponsibilities as well as an officer's rights and responsibilities.

By teaching people what to expect when encountering the police and educating them as to their true rights and responsibili-ties, we bridge the disconnect associated with how one THINKS an officer should act and how they are trained to act. By reducing the number of unmet expectations based on untrue beliefs, we may be able to reduce some of the toxic vitriol spewed toward the profession of policing. This would necessarily decrease negative encounters with police and help create the change we all desire.

Chapter 12
BE YOUR BROTHER'S KEEPER

The intent of this writing is twofold. First, I wanted to give you all an insight into the struggles of someone struggling with Post-Traumatic Stress Disorder. Second, I wanted to bring attention to failings withing the law enforcement profession. To do this I used personal experiences (both good and bad) gathered over 13 years in law enforcement. Because of the decisions the man who shot me made on May 7th, 2016, I was shot, eventually fired, lost my family, my house, my livelihood, and my identity.

Since my shooting, I have been repeatedly asked, "Do you regret being a police officer?" This question has plagued me and until recently, I did not have an answer. On the one hand, I believe I had a positive impact in keeping my community safe. I know the names of people who are only alive because of the actions I took while performing my duty. I have been there when people took their last breath and comforted their loved ones as they grieved the loss. I have seen what good people with good hearts can do in the name of keeping their communities safe. On the other hand, the vitriol and hatred spewed toward our police officers is overwhelming. It was not until I began this writing, that I believe I have found my answer.

No, I do not regret becoming a police officer. However, given the "war on police," I do not know why anyone would choose to subject themselves to this profession and all it entails. Everything in life is decided through a process of determining the benefits and risks associated with any given task. As long as an action produces more benefit than cost, we tend to believe the action worthwhile. We have created a situation in which the risks of being a police officer far outweigh the benefits associated with the profession. But It is not too late.

After reading my suggestions for change, you may believe they are underdeveloped or lacking in some fashion. I hope this is the case! I hope this writing inspires you to develop a more complete model by which we can help end the negativity toward policing, bridge the gap between policing and our citizenry, and help stem the growing suicide epidemic with the law enforcement community.

Regardless of your opinions on my specific suggestions regarding change, I think it is obvious that change is needed to protect our law enforcement professionals. We need to protect officers from administrators who are more concerned with their budget rather than the injured officer's long-term wellbeing; We need to create educational initiatives to close the widening gap between what a person thinks their rights to be and what they actually are; we need to stop the villainization of police in our media. Until we can address these issues, I fear for the future of policing and the safety for each of you who choose the noble profession.

How do we begin to change the profession of law enforcement to protect the men and women who risk their lives to protect us? I will leave you with one last story:

Recently, Operation Enduring Warrior honored me and multiple other injured law enforcement officers and military vets at the WarX obstacle course race in Ohio. Operation Enduring Warrior brought 11 honorees (with varying types of injuries) and 25 "masked athletes" (in support of the honorees.) In addition, over 100 Community Ambassadors spent their own money and volunteered their time to ensure the organization's mission could succeed and that every honoree was cared for to the best of their ability.

I arrived on midday Friday. As I was strolling about the WarX compound, one of the Community Ambassadors stopped me. He spoke to me like we had known each other for decades. He used my first name and spoke about his wife as if the three of us had eaten dinner the night before. I was embarrassed because I did not recognize him. I smiled shook his hand and searched my memory trying to identify how this man knew me and why he knew me so well. He made a couple of comments regarding some of my social media activity, so I assumed he knew me through his being one of the Community Ambassadors and he was simply being friendly and kind (like they all are). After a little banter, he wished me luck on the obstacle course, and we parted ways.

The next morning, I woke earlier than most eager to begin the event. I knew from participation the year prior, there were to be loud explosions and sustained gunfire. I participated in that event the year prior, as a form of Exposure Therapy. The idea was to renormalize me to the sound of gunfire through exposure to gunfire. Although it was not easy, I credit my participation in this event and the support given by all parties involved with my renewed interests in shooting sports.

The kindness and genuine interest the Community Ambassador I had spoken with the night before, stuck with me so I sought him out to speak with him before the race. I found him happy and encouraging to everyone he spoke with. He laughed, he joked, he offered to help in any way he could. He seemed to really care about the honorees and seemed to want to do anything in his power to help. I found his energy inspiring. I shook his hand as he wished me luck on the course for a second time. I thanked him and went about participating in the event.

The WarX obstacle course was grueling. It was over 6 miles long, contained over 50 obstacles, and was set up to simulate a war-time environment. As part of the event, we were given a mission. We were under attack and needed to escape the compound. The only way out was the path through the course. After a brief introduction from the WarX host, the explosions and gunfire erupted all around. There were both small caliber and large-caliber weapons. Men with assault rifles roamed the woods in ATVs as we began the course, attempting to find our way out.

We completed the course as a team around five in the afternoon. The heat index had been around 102 degrees and we were all exhausted. While exhausted, I felt a level of accomplishment I can only describe as elating. Since my shooting, my grip strength suffered and because of this, I was unable to complete tasks that required me to support my body weight by my right arm. At this event, my grip strength not only held but I was able to climb a 20-foot rope for the first time since my injury. Although exhausted, I felt like I could accomplish anything.

Shortly after the race, as darkness fell, our hosts lit a bonfire. This bonfire was intended to create a space for us all to sit and talk about our shared experiences as well as get to know one another in a more intimate way. The Community Ambassador who I had spoken with before the race, his wife and about six other people were already enjoying the fire when I arrived. We laughed and joked about random things and I continued to rack my brain trying to remember if we had met and why they seemed to know me so well.

After a bit of visiting around the fire, talking about everything from politics to "war stories," I was fairly sure they only knew me because I was an honoree with Operation Enduring Warrior and due to my Facebook presence. I was exhausted and was ready to head to bed. I stood up and thanked the man and his wife for their support and their energy. I also made mention it was nice to meet them.

It was then, that the man's wife spoke up. She stated, "You don't remember do you... oh I'm really going to make you feel like an ass." I knew I had put my foot in my mouth instantly. She then asked, "are you ready to feel like an ass?"

The three of us joked and I told her, "lay it on me."

The man's wife explained they were from the Tennessee area and two years ago they came out to the Warrior's Challenge obstacle course race in Kuttawa, Kentucky. That was my first event with Operation Enduring Warrior. After completing the event in Kentucky, the hosts had a stage set up and brought in a couple of bands. Between the openers and the headliners, they asked Operation Enduring Warrior representatives to speak to the crowd about the organization and what their mission was.

They also asked that I share a couple of words about who I was, what I had experienced, and how the organization had helped me. I spoke about many of the problems I wrote in this book. I spoke about my shooting, my firing, many of the struggles associated with Post-Traumatic Stress Disorder, and suicide. I challenged everyone who was struggling or knew someone who may be struggling, to speak up and seek help. This was only my second time speaking on such topics in front of a crowd and I remember being extremely nervous. I was not sure if anyone had heard my message, but I figured if just one person listened and sought out help, any anxiety and/or stress associated with my discussing my issues would be worth it.

I interrupted the woman as she explained how she first met

me. I remembered she and her husband walking up and speaking with me after I left the stage, but I could not remember the specifics of our conversation. Then she said it:

"After hearing your speech, what you went through, and what you were dealing with, my husband opened up about his experiences and asked for help."

She went on to explain how she had known for some time her husband was struggling due to his military service, but she was unsure of how to help or how to approach the situation to suggest he seek out help. It was only after seeing me stand up and admit to my own issues, was this man able to find the courage within himself to do the same.

Since our first meeting, in Kentucky, the man has entered counseling and is seeking help for many of the same issues I spoke about. Now the couple sat here in front of me while crediting my speech in Kentucky, a speech I barely remember giving, with pushing the man to get help and save his life.

We never know when our words or actions could reach a person who really needs help. Could your speaking up potentially save the life of a brother, a sister, your father, or your mother? If there is the slightest chance you can help, is it not worth a try?

EPILOGUE

It has now been over four years since I was attacked, beaten, and shot. I continue to bear the torment this man chose to impose upon me. I deal with near-constant pain in my right arm, much like the pain one feels when they hit their funny bone. Some days I am able to ignore the pain and other days the pain is so intense it brings me to tears. I am regularly haunted by memories, nightmares, and intrusive thoughts, most of which I have no ability to control. Through my attacker's decisions, my life changed so drastically, I am scarcely a mirage of the person I once was.

When a person goes through life-changing trauma, it is common for the person's outlook on life to change. They may become more jaded, less trusting, or even seem to become a whole new person all-together. Coping is different for each person, however, I found helping others navigate the "landmines" associated with Post-Traumatic Stress Disorder has become the single most beneficial mechanism by which I have found the strength to continue.

Helping others can take many forms. For some, it may mean volunteering at a local shelter, food bank, or some other charitable organization. For others, help may come in the form of personal interactions with those the person knows to be suffering. For me, it took the form of writing and speaking about my struggles to anyone who would listen, so others may find a path to help them cope with their individual symptoms associated with Post-Traumatic stress disorder.

Regardless of the method you choose, helping others who suffer is beneficial for all involved. When one is being aided through difficult times, they tend to admire the person who has set out to help them. This admiration helps create a level of responsibility the sufferer now feels toward the ones helping them. One can use this sense of responsibility to others (and to themselves) to help create healthy routines, motivate an individual to seek out professional help, and most importantly, ensure the individual never feels alone in their struggles.

In addition to the benefits, the suffer feels in this relationship, the individual attempting to help gets to feel a sense of purpose. This sense of purpose can help create a sense of responsibility to the one suffering, better allowing the helper to face their own problems and seek out a healthy coping mechanism. As the helper continues to help, they learn new coping mechanisms and new ways to battle the demons, which they can then apply to their own situation.

We are living in a time where there is an active "war on police." Police officers are targeted simply because they wear the uniform. The individuals who swore to protect us are now being demonized and attacked while our communities and many in our government refuse to help. We are seeing riots, death, and destruction all around us while our police officers continue to risk everything to keep evil at bay. It is very demoralizing to continually try and do the right thing when one is treated in such a way. With all of the external hate spewed at us, we must stick together and break our collective refusal to address mental health issues within law enforcement. We must make it okay to say, "I need help."

Our officers need support from our government. Too often,

the police are blamed for crime rates, drug issues, racism, etc., all as political talking points. In recent months, this has materialized in the "defund the police movement." Contrary to this movement's rhetoric, investment in our policing agencies is the only mechanism by which we may end the police suicide epidemic and create more trust between our police officers and the communities they swear their lives to protect. The police cannot continue to be the scapegoat for all of society's problems. I believe this begins with public education regarding individual rights and responsibilities under the law.

The men and women who put on the uniform do so out of love for their community and fellow man. Instead of disparaging our police officers, we must find a way to come together to ensure our officers have all the tools needed to guarantee they can keep our communities safe, make it home to their families after each shift, and continue to fight against the demons associated with police work.

Last night, I found myself woken suddenly. I was covered in sweat, my heart was racing, and I had a horribly uneasy feeling radiating through my entire body. I knew I had a nightmare, but I did not recall the specifics. After an hour or more, aided by doctor prescribed medications, I found sleep.

I awoke this morning with a tremendous feeling of impending doom. I did not want to get out of bed and fear was pushing me to lock myself away for the day. This feeling made me incredibly uneasy. Every shadow, every person I see, every motion I catch out of the corner of my eye feels like a threat. In years past, I would have self-medicated using alcohol to the point of unconsciousness. Today, however, I went to the gym, I took a shower, and I wrote this.

Writing this book has been very difficult for me. It has forced me to look deeper into myself and the circumstances which led me to where I am now. Each time I read the words I put on paper

I feel the pain just as vividly as when the incidents occurred.

I do not expect one to read this book and have some sort of epiphany. My assumption is that if you are reading this, it is because you have already recognized a problem and you are looking for ways to create change, either in yourself or for someone you love.

There is a stigma surrounding mental health issues in law enforcement. The mere mention of a mental health struggle can cause disastrous consequences to an officer's career and in doing so, their family. Not talking about these issues can lead to marital problems, alcohol issues, or worse...suicide.

Through my struggles with Post-Traumatic Stress Disorder, I felt the depths of the darkness that is depression. I have nearly committed suicide on two occasions, thinking it was the only way to make the pain stop. I used alcohol and other unhealthy coping mechanisms to help quiet the storm in my mind. I only began to heal when I discovered a new purpose.

Helping my brothers or sisters who struggle has allowed me to step outside myself, if only for a moment. In these moments, I see a clear path to a happy and self-fulfilling life. A life where I live with the symptoms, but my symptoms do not control my life.

We all recognize the insurmountable hurdles in front of us. How can we expect any individual to begin to make the needed societal and cultural changes?

By reaching one person at a time...

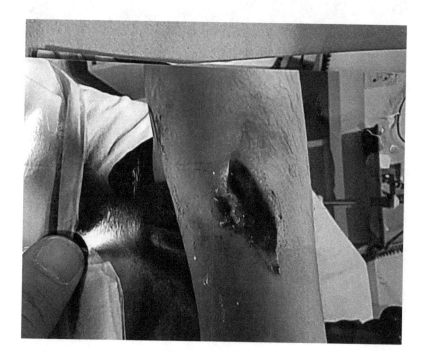

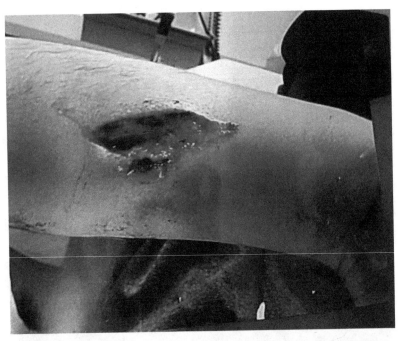

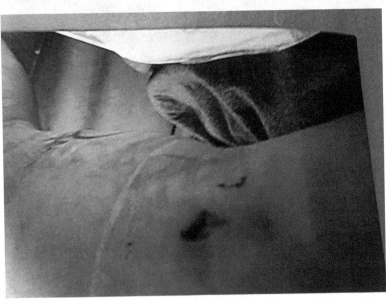